ICONS

SOUTH AFRICAN STYLE

SOUTH AFR

Exteriors   Interiors

ICAN STYLE
Details

PHOTOS **Deidi von Schaewen**
EDITOR **Angelika Taschen**

TASCHEN

KÖLN LONDON LOS ANGELES MADRID PARIS TOKYO

Front cover: Between sea and sky: Jean-Marc Lederman's radiant blue pool.
Couverture : Entre ciel et terre : le bleu lumineux de la piscine de Jean-Marc Lederman.
Umschlagvorderseite: Zwischen Himmel und Meer: Der leuchtend blaue Pool von Jean-Marc Lederman.

Back cover: A cordial welcome: in front of a small shop in a Cape Town township.
Dos de Couverture : Bienvenue : devant une petite boutique des bidonvilles du Cap.
Umschlagrückseite: Herzlich willkommen: Vor einem kleinen Laden in den Townships von Kapstadt.

Also available from TASCHEN:

Inside Africa
912 pages
3–8228–5771–8

To stay informed about upcoming TASCHEN titles, please request our magazine at www.taschen.com/magazine or write to TASCHEN, Hohenzollernring 53, D-50672 Cologne, Germany, contact@taschen.com, Fax: +49-221-254919. We will be happy to send you a free copy of our magazine which is filled with information about all of our books.

Edited by Angelika Taschen, Berlin
Layout and project management by Stephanie Bischoff, Cologne
Text edited by Christiane Reiter, Berlin
Lithography by Horst Neuzner, Cologne
English translation by Pauline Cumbers, Frankfurt am Main
French translation by Anne Charrière, Croissy/Seine

Printed in Italy
ISBN 3–8228–3913–2

CONTENTS SOMMAIRE INHALT

Beaches on which the ebb and flow of the tide paints silver lines, mountains dramatically enveloped in swathes of cloud, the exotic green shades, the sounds and smells of the bush: South Africa is like a setting for a film. It has natural scenarios full of magic and mysticism, and enticing plots of building land which people have dreamed of all their life. Here, architects discover their paradise – including snakes. The Cape of Good Hope offers a million possibilities, but which one does justice to this wonderful country, takes into account its turbulent and often bloody history, suits the present and at the same time points the way to the future? Designers in South Africa have to achieve a balancing act between art and nature, tradition and modernism, knowledge and intuition, have to give these much thought and yet not allow them to thwart their plans. And they do this with a mixture of wholehearted pride for their homeland (or the homeland of their choice) and a

ON THE CAPE OF GOOD HOPE
Christiane Reiter

Des plages où la marée dessine des bandes argentées ; des montagnes enveloppées de voiles nébuleux dramatiques ; la brousse, qui fascine par ses tons verts, ses bruits et ses odeurs étranges : l'Afrique du Sud est un monde en soi, qui a tout d'un décor de théâtre, avec ses spectacles naturels magiques et mystiques. Nous y sommes attirés par des terrains dont nous avons rêvé depuis longtemps, et les architectes y trouvent leur paradis – serpents compris : car au Cap de Bonne-Espérance, les possibilités sont légion ; quelle sera celle qui fera honneur à ce magnifique pays, respectera son passé varié et souvent sanguinaire, s'accordera avec le présent et montrera le chemin de l'avenir ? C'est de ce grand écart entre art et nature, tradition et modernité, savoir et intuition, dont les designers doivent se montrer capables en Afrique du Sud. Réfléchir sur de nombreuses questions sans se laisser dérouter – ils y parviennent avec un mélange de fierté absolue pour leur patrie (d'adoption) et une insouciance qui paraît parfois naïve, voire excentrique.

Strände, auf die die Flut silbrige Streifen malt, Berge, die sich in dramatische Nebelkleider hüllen, Buschland, das mit fremdartigen Grüntönen, Geräuschen und Gerüchen fasziniert: Südafrika ist ein Reich wie eine Kinokulisse. Es besitzt Naturschauplätze voller Magie und Mystik, es lockt mit Grundstücken, von denen man ein Leben lang träumt, und Architekten finden hier ihr Paradies – inklusive Schlangen: Denn am Kap der Guten Hoffnung eröffnen sich eine Million Möglichkeiten; welche ist die eine, die diesem wunderschönen Land gerecht wird, die Rücksicht auf seine wechselvolle und oft blutige Vergangenheit nimmt, die in die Gegenwart passt und den Menschen den Weg in die Zukunft zeigt? Es ist ein Spagat zwischen Kunst und Natur, zwischen Tradition und Moderne, zwischen Wissen und Intuition, den Designer in Südafrika bewältigen müssen. Vieles bedenken und sich dennoch nicht aus dem Konzept bringen lassen – das schaffen sie mit einer Mischung aus unbedingtem Stolz auf ihre (Wahl)Heimat und einer Unbeschwertheit, die manchmal naiv

carefree attitude that sometimes seems naive, even eccentric. For example, the cottage in Greyton that combines the plush style of the British country-manor with the brilliance of the rainbow nation that is South Africa; then there is the villa near Cape Town that is almost submerged in intoxicating colours and styles and whose pool is guarded by a siren. Enthroned up on the hills outside Johannesburg is a miniature Versailles, while a manor in Stellenbosch revitalizes the Cape Dutch style, and a lodge in the Safari-look even brings a touch of wild life into the city. Critics like to reproach the architects of such buildings with indulging their vanity in playful escapades and creating a totally unreal image of Africa, right next to the still existing townships. Yet despite such crass opposites, architects and designers can also help to give novel hues and fresh nuances to a country where until recently there was only black and white.

On découvre ainsi le cottage de Greyton, qui allie le style de la maison de campagne douillette britannique avec la force lumineuse de la nation arc-en-ciel, comme on appelle l'Afrique du Sud ; ou bien cette Villa près du Cap, noyée dans une ivresse de couleurs et de styles, qui confie sa piscine à la garde d'une sirène ; ou ce Versailles en miniature qui trône parmi les collines de Johannesburg ; ou encore un manoir à Stellenbosch qui fait revivre le style 'Cap-hollandais' ; ou enfin un pavillon au look Safari, qui introduit un soupçon de vie sauvage au cœur de la ville. Les critiques reprochent ici volontiers aux architectes de donner libre cours à leur vanité en construisant une image de l'Afrique complètement étrangère à la réalité, tout près des bidonvilles qui existent encore. Mais au-delà du choc de ces contradictions, l'architecture et le design peuvent aussi aider à apporter des couleurs fraîches et de nouvelles nuances dans un pays où, jusqu'à récemment, seuls existaient le noir et le blanc.

oder sogar exzentrisch wirkt. Da ist zum Beispiel das Cottage in Greyton, das britisch-plüschigen Landhausstil mit der Leuchtkraft der Regenbogennation Südafrika verbindet; da ist die Villa bei Kapstadt, die im Rausch der Farben und Stile ertrinkt und ihren Pool von einer Sirene bewachen lässt. Da thront ein Versailles en miniature in den Hügeln bei Johannesburg, da lässt ein Herrenhaus in Stellenbosch den Cape-Dutch-Style wieder aufleben, und da bringt eine Lodge im Safari-Look einen Hauch von Wildlife in die Stadt. Kritiker werfen den Architekten solcher Bauten gerne vor, sie tobten sich auf einem Spielplatz der Eitelkeiten aus und konstruierten ein völlig realitätsfernes Bild Afrikas in unmittelbarer Nähe der noch immer existierenden Townships. Doch aller aufeinander prallenden Gegensätze zum Trotz: Auch Architektur und Design können dabei helfen, frische Farben und neue Nuancen in ein Land zu bringen, in dem bis vor kurzem nur Schwarz und Weiß existierten.

"…The farm is called Voelfontein, Bird Fountain; he loves every stone of it, every bush, every blade of grass, he loves the birds that gave its name…"

J.M. Coetzee, in *Boyhood. Scenes from a Provincial Life*

«…La ferme s'appelle Voëlfontein, fontaine aux oiseaux ; il y aime chaque pierre, chaque buisson, chaque brin d'herbe, il aime les oiseaux qui lui donnent son nom…»

J.M. Coetzee, dans *Scènes de la vie d'un jeune garçon*

»…Die Farm heißt Voëlfontein, Vogelquelle; er liebt jeden Stein dort, jeden Busch, jeden Grashalm, er liebt die Vögel, nach denen sie benannt ist…«

J.M. Coetzee, in *Der Junge. Eine afrikanische Kindheit*

EXTERIORS

Extérieurs   Aussichten

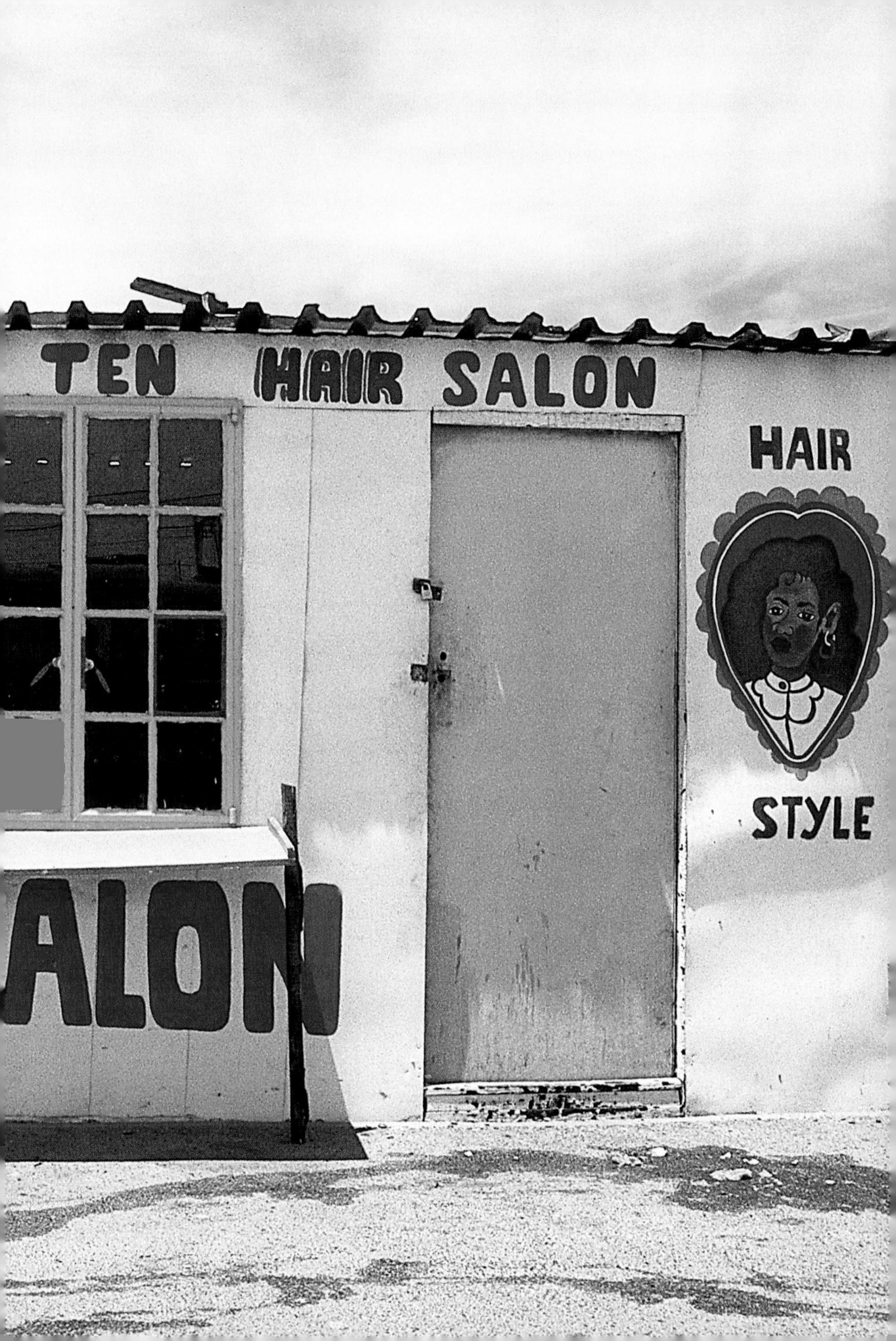
TEN HAIR SALON
HAIR
STYLE
ALON

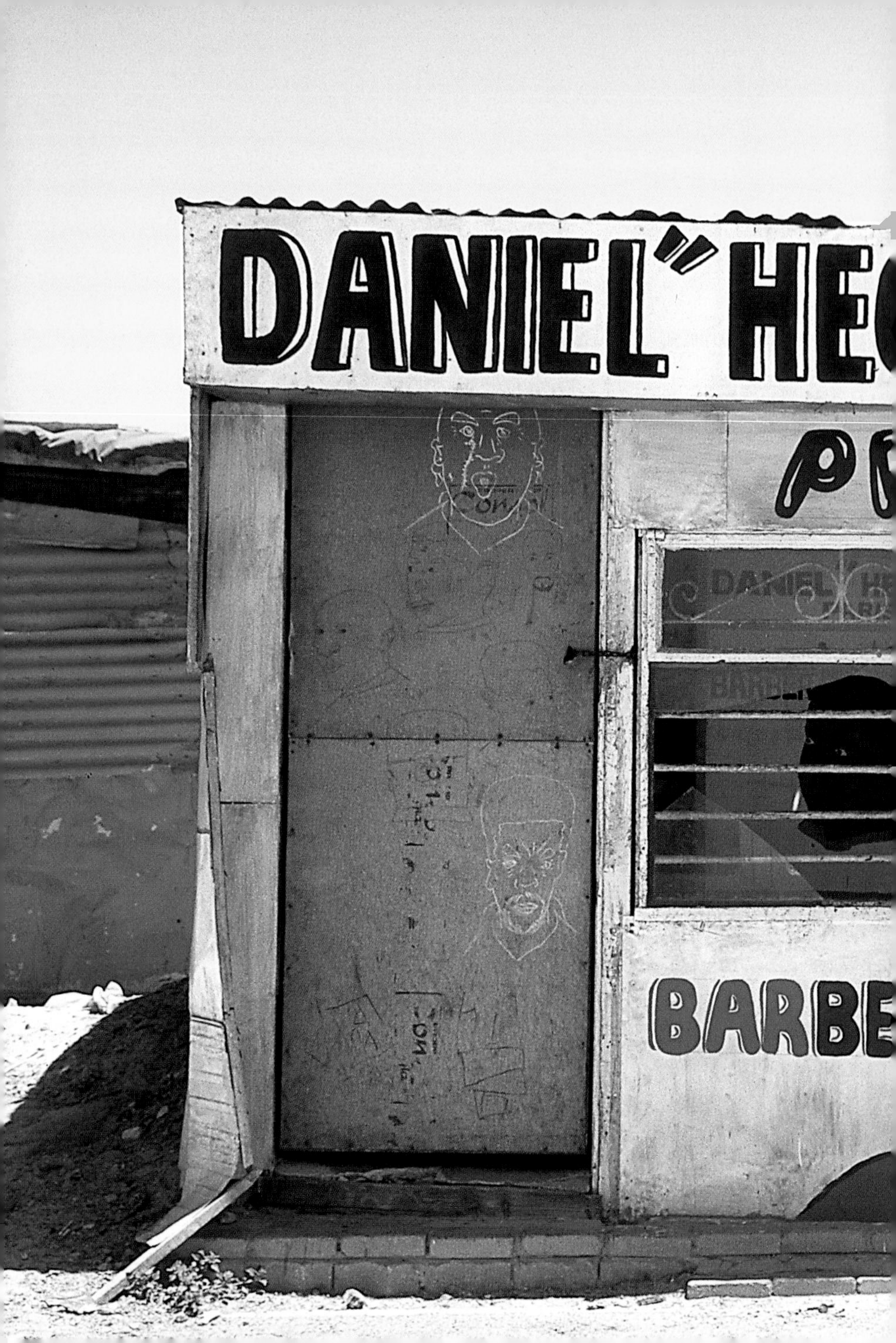
DANIEL" HE
BARBE

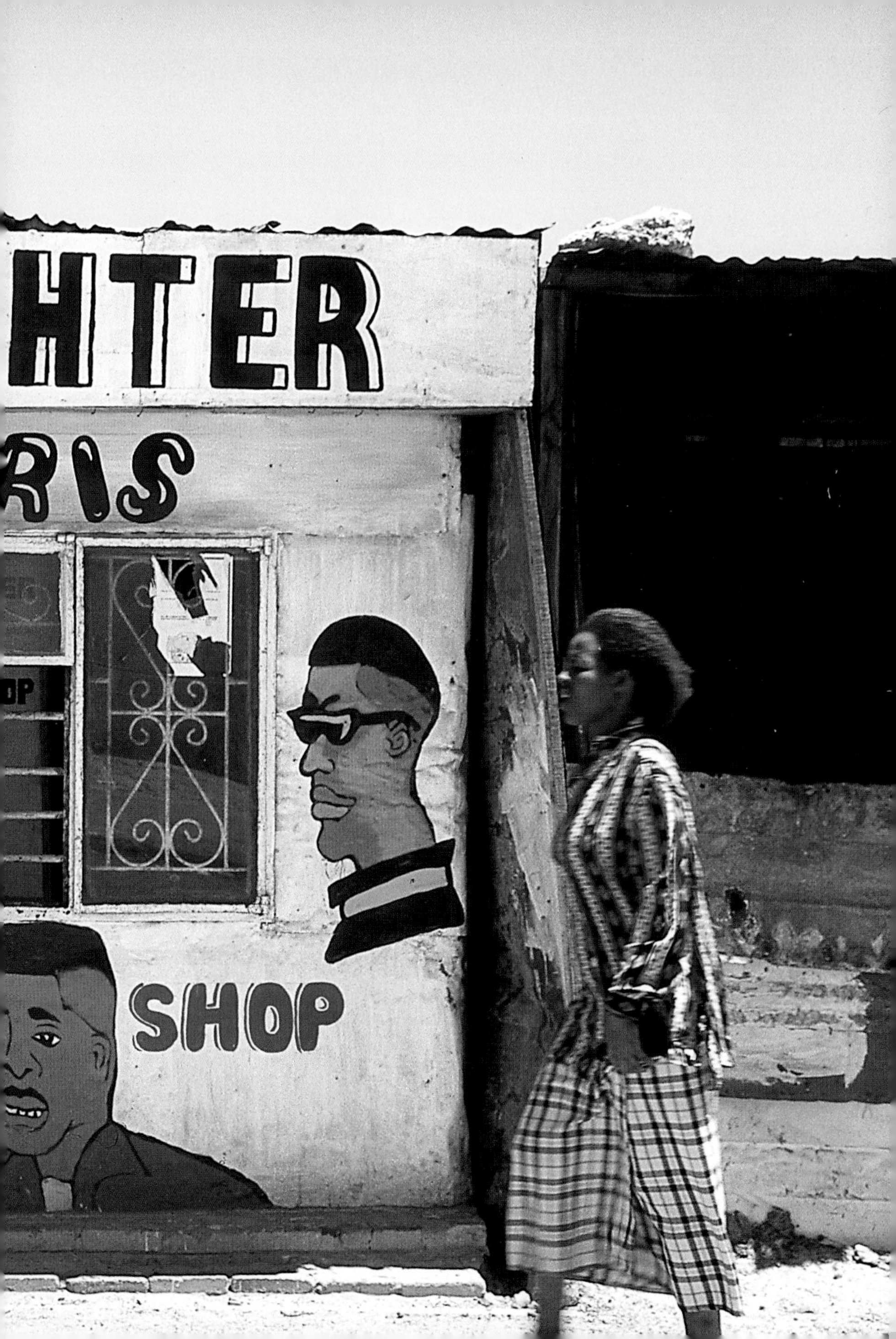
HTER
RIS
SHOP

10/11 A family outing: a herd of elephants in the South African bush. *Excursion en famille : un troupeau d'éléphants dans la brousse sud-africaine.* Familienausflug: Eine Elefantenherde im südafrikanischen Busch.

12/13 At close quarters with animals: in the architect Silvio Rech's private lodge Lutopi. *Contact étroit avec les animaux : dans le lodge privé Lutopi de l'architecte Silvio Rech.* Auf Tuchfühlung mit den Tieren: In der Privatlodge Lutopi des Architekten Silvio Rech.

14/15 Freedom of form: imaginative buildings on the grounds of Lutopi. *Liberté de forme : constructions pleines d'imagination sur le terrain de Lutopi.* Freiheit der Form: Fantasievolle Bauten auf dem Gelände von Lutopi.

16/17 Like a film set: an artwork in Lutopi – with a view of the Drakensberge. *Décors de cinéma : une œuvre d'art à Lutopi – avec vue sur les monts Draken.* Kinotaugliche Kulisse: Ein Kunstwerk in Lutopi – mit Blick auf die Drakensberge.

18/19 A modern water hole: the beautifully situated pool in Camp 5, Makalali. *Point d'eau des temps modernes : site de rêve pour la piscine du Camp 5, Makalali.* Wasserloch der Neuzeit: Der traumhaft gelegene Pool des Camp 5, Makalali.

20/21 Lodge with a view: a terrace in Camp 5 hidden by Jackalberry trees. *Lodge avec vue : sur une terrasse cachée dans les ébénier d'Afrique, au Camp 5.* Lodge mit Aussicht: Auf einer in den Jackalberry-Bäumen versteckten Terrasse des Camp 5.

22/23 Sleeping al fresco: a luxurious place for the night in Camp 5. *Dormir à la belle étoile : un gîte luxueux pour la nuit, au Camp 5.* Schlafen unter freiem Himmel: Ein luxuriöses Nachtlager im Camp 5.

24/25 A guest of Sleeping Beauty: Bathafarh Farm near Johannesburg. *Hôtes de la Belle au bois dormant : la ferme Bathafarh, près de Johannesburg.* Zu Gast bei Dornröschen: Das Märchenschloss Bathafarh Farm, bei Johannesburg.

26/27 Homage to Versailles: pond with Trianon columns in the park of Bathafarh Farm. *Hommage à Versailles : bassin d'eau et colonnes style Trianon, dans le parc de la ferme Bathafarh.* Hommage an Versailles: Wasserbecken mit Trianon-Säulen im Park der Bathafarh Farm.

28/29 The drama of nature: in front of the door of Beezy Bailey's house, Cape Town. *Mise en scène dramatique de l'espace naturel, juste devant la porte : la maison de Beezy Bailey, Le Cap.* Dramatisch inszenierte Natur direkt vor der Tür: Das Haus von Beezy Bailey, Kapstadt.

30/31 A host of co-inhabitants: in front of the villa "Meerlust", Stellenbosch. *Toute une troupe de colocataires : devant la Villa « Meerlust » à Stellenbosch.* Eine ganze Schar von Mitbewohnern: Vor der Villa »Meerlust«, Stellenbosch.

32/33 Exemplary: an Ndebele house in Mpumalanga province. *Exemplaire : une maison Ndebele, dans la province de Mpumalanga.* Mustergültig: Ein Haus der Ndebele, in der Provinz Mpumalanga.

34/35 Modern motifs in a traditional technique: on the walls of a round Ndebele house. *Technique traditionnelle et motifs modernes : au mur d'une construction ronde Ndebele.* Traditionelle Technik und moderne Motive: An den Wänden eines Rundbaus der Ndebele.

36/37 Protection from evil spirits: colourful walls around an Ndebele house. *Protection contre les mauvais esprits : des murs hauts en couleurs autour d'une maison Ndebele.* Schutz vor bösen Geistern: Bunt bemalte Mauern rund um ein Haus der Ndebele.

38/39 A quick trim: at the hairdresser's salon in a Cape Town township. *Coupe rapide : un salon de coiffure dans les bidonvilles du Cap.* Für den schnellen Schnitt: Ein Friseursalon in den Townships von Kapstadt.

40/41 Longing for big names: a fashion boutique in a Cape Town township. *Nostalgie des grands noms : une boutique de mode dans les bidonvilles du Cap.* Sehnsucht nach großen Namen: Eine Modeboutique in den Townships von Kapstadt.

42/43 The blue house: Malcolm Kluk's home in a former working-class quarter of Cape Town. *La maison bleue : chez Malcolm Kluk, dans un ancien quartier d'ouvriers du Cap.* Das blaue Haus: Bei Malcolm Kluk, in einem ehemaligen Arbeiterviertel von Kapstadt.

44/45 The blue hour: the idyllic inner courtyard of Malcolm Kluk's house. *L'« heure bleue » dans la cour intérieure idyllique de la maison de Malcolm Kluk.* »Blaue Stunden«: Im idyllischen Innenhof von Malcolm Kluk.

46/47 Terraced: Jean-Marc Lederman's gardens in Llandudno. *En terrasse : les jardins de Jean-Marc Lederman à Llandudno.* Terrassenförmig angelegt: Die Gärten von Jean-Marc Lederman in Llandudno.

48/49 In the style of Frank Lloyd Wright: Jean-Marc Lederman's house and pool. *Dans le style de Frank Lloyd Wright : la maison et la piscine de Jean-Marc Lederman.* Im Stil von Frank Lloyd Wright: Haus und Pool von Jean-Marc Lederman.

50/51 Between sea and sky: Jean-Marc Lederman's radiant blue pool. *Entre ciel et terre : le bleu lumineux de la piscine de Jean-Marc Lederman.* Zwischen Himmel und Meer: Der leuchtend blaue Pool von Jean-Marc Lederman.

52/53 Life on the beach: a penguin colony on the coast of South Africa. *Vie de plage en noir et blanc : une colonie de pingouins sur la côte de l'Afrique du Sud.* Strandleben in Schwarz und Weiß: Eine Pinguinkolonie an Südafrikas Küste.

54/55 Bathed in colour: that magical moment between day and night. *Plongée dans la couleur : l'instant magique entre le jour et la nuit.* In Farbe getaucht: Der magische Moment zwischen Tag und Nacht.

"...We woke at dawn to find the world a glistening, silvery-grey place full of exuberant noise..."

Kobie Krüger, in *The Wilderness Family*

«...Nous nous sommes réveillés au petit jour, et le monde devant nos fenêtres était un paradis vert argenté, plein de voix d'animaux jubilantes...»

Kobie Krüger, dans *The Wilderness Family*

»...Wir erwachten in der Morgendämmerung, und die Welt vor unserem Fenster war ein silbrig grünes Paradies voller überschwänglicher Tierstimmen...«

Kobie Krüger, in *Ich trage Afrika im Herzen*

INTERIORS

Intérieurs   Einsichten

60/61 A fine mix: the traditional and at the same time modern salon in the private lodge. *Mélange de matériaux : le salon à la fois traditionnel et moderne du lodge privé .* Materialmix: Im traditionell und modern zugleich gestalteten Salon der Privatlodge.

62/63 Under observation: the billiard room at the private Lutopi lodge. *Sous surveillance : la salle de billard du loge privé Lutopi.* Unter Beobachtung: Das Billard-Zimmer in der Privatlodge Lutopi.

64/65 Bathing above the trees: a favourite spot in Pierre Lombart's house. *Se baigner audessus des arbres : un endroit apprécié dans la maison de Pierre Lombart.* Baden hoch über den Bäumen: Lieblingsplatz im Haus von Pierre Lombart.

66/67 The art of living and reading: room with a panoramic view in Pierre Lombart's home. *L'art de vivre et de lire : une pièce avec vue panoramique chez Pierre Lombart.* Leben und Lesen: Ein kunstvoll gestalteter Raum mit Panorama bei Pierre Lombart.

68/69 Lofty space: Pierre Lombart's transparently designed house, Johannesburg. *Pièces hautes : dans la maison de Pierre Lombart, Johannesburg — mot clé : la transparence.* Hohe Räume: Im transparent gestalteten Haus von Pierre Lombart, Johannesburg.

70/71 Minimalist: simple white seating unit in Jean-Marc Lederman's house. *Minimalistes : de sobres canapés blancs chez Jean-Marc Lederman.* Minimalistisch: Schlichte weiße Sofas bei Jean-Marc Lederman.

72/73 Open spaces: bathroom, resting area and living room at Jean-Marc Lederman's. *Espaces ouverts : salle de bains, coin repos et salon chez Jean-Marc Lederman.* Offene Räume: Bad, Ruhebereich und Wohnzimmer bei Jean-Marc Lederman.

74/75 Art everywhere: sculptures and colourful fabrics in Jean-Marc Lederman's house. *Tout est art : sculptures et étoffes colorées, chez Jean-Marc Lederman, Llandudno.* Alles ist Kunst: Skulpturen und bunte Stoffe bei Jean-Marc Lederman, Llandudno.

76/77 Essentially graphic: in an Ndebele house, Mpumalanga province. *Graphique, un principe : dans une maison Ndebele, province de Mpumalanga.* Grafik als Prinzip: In einem Haus der Ndebele, Provinz Mpumalanga.

78/79 A feast of colours and forms: an Ndebele bedroom. *Une fête des formes et des couleurs : chambre à coucher Ndebele.* Ein Fest der Farben und Formen: Ein Schlafzimmer der Ndebele.

80/81 A neat solution: the bathroom of Ndebele artist Esther Mahlangu. *Claire et nette : la salle de bains de l'artiste Ndebele Esther Mahlangu.* Eine saubere Sache: Im Bad der Ndebele-Künstlerin Esther Mahlangu.

82/83 Expansive: a plush bedroom in a township. *Prise de possession : une chambre à coucher douillette des bidonvilles.* Besitz ergreifend: In einem plüschig gestalteten Schlafzimmer in den Townships.

84/85 Well insulated: a kitchen in a Cape Town township. *Bien isolée : une cuisine dans les bidonvilles du Cap.* Gut isoliert: Eine Küche in den Townships von Kapstadt.

86/87 Recycled: wallpaper made of packaging, in a Cape Town township. *Recyclage : papier peint en matériaux d'emballage, dans les bidonvilles du Cap.* Wieder verwertet: Tapeten aus Verpackungsmaterial, in den Townships von Kapstadt.

88/89 Wallpaper variations: in a Cape Town township. *Papier peint style recyclé : dans les bidonvilles du Cap.* Tapete im Recyclinglook: In den Townships von Kapstadt.

90/91 Carefully piled: another "recycling kitchen" in a township. *Soigneusement empilés : une autre « cuisine recyclée » des bidonvilles.* Sorgfältig gestapelt: Eine weitere »Recycling-Küche« in den Townships.

92/93 With the compliments of Knorr: a quiet corner in a township. *Avec les compliments de Knorr : un coin tranquille dans les bidonvilles.* Knorr lässt grüßen: Eine ruhige Ecke in den Townships.

94/95 Brilliant colours: in Mike Donkins' rustic cottage in Greyton. *Couleurs lumineuses : la maison de campagne rustique de Mike Donkins, Greyton.* Farben mit Leuchtkraft: Im rustikalen Cottage von Mike Donkins, Greyton.

96/97 Artful kitsch: Beezy Bailey's eccentrically designed house, Cape Town. *Kitsch artistique : la demeure au design excentrique de Beezy Bailey, Le Cap.* Kunstvoller Kitsch: Im exzentrisch designten Haus von Beezy Bailey, Kapstadt.

98/99 Framed in blue: Beezy Bailey's kitchen. *Encadrée de bleu : la cuisine de Beezy Bailey.* Blau umrahmt: Die Küche von Beezy Bailey.

100/101 Best wishes: Malcolm Kluk's living room, Cape Town. *Meilleurs vœux : le salon de Malcolm Kluk, au Cap.* Mit allen guten Wünschen: Das Wohnzimmer von Malcolm Kluk, Kapstadt.

102/103 Stripes: Malcolm Kluk's harmonious bedroom. *Design à rayures : effets harmonieux dans la chambre à coucher de Malcolm Kluk.* Im Streifendesgin: Das harmonisch wirkende Schlafzimmer von Malcolm Kluk.

104/105 Fireplace: at Shahn and Alice Rowe's house, Johannesburg. *Coin du feu : la cheminée dans la maison de Shahn et Alice Rowe, Johannesburg.* Feuerstelle: Der Kamin im Haus von Shahn und Alice Rowe, Johannesburg.

106/107 Souvenirs: Shahn and Alice Rowe's favourite items from Africa. *Collection de souvenirs : Les objets africains préférés de Shahn et Alice Rowe.* Gesammelte Souvenirs: Lieblingsstücke aus Afrika; bei Shahn und Alice Rowe.

108/109 Africa meets Art Deco: the salon at the home of Tracy Rushmere and Peter Maltbie. *L'Afrique à la rencontre de l'Art-Déco : le salon de Tracy Rushmere et Peter Maltbie.* Africa meets Art-déco: Im Salon von Tracy Rushmere und Peter Maltbie.

110/111 Spacious: the dining and living room of Tracy Rushmere and Peter Maltbie. *Vaste et claire: la salle à manger-salon de Tracy Rushmere et Peter Maltbie.* Raum und Weite: Das Ess- und Wohnzimmer von Tracy Rushmere und Peter Maltbie.

112/113 Multi-cultural: Rushmere & Maltbie's atmospheric bedroom. *Atmosphère multiculturelle : la chambre à coucher de Rushmere et Maltbie.* Multikulturelle Atmosphäre: Im Schlafzimmer des Paares Rushmere & Maltbie.

114/115 A touch of green: "De oude Schuur", Craig Port's loft, Cape Town. *Accent vert : le loft « De oude Schuur » de Craig Port, Le Cap.* Grüner Akzent: Im Loft »De oude Schuur« von Craig Port, Kapstadt.

116/117 Seating area: white-covered sofas and old club armchairs at Craig Port's home. *Détente: sofas habillés de blanc et vieux fauteuils club chez Craig Port.* Sitzgelegenheiten: Weiß bezogene Sofas und alte Clubsessel bei Craig Port.

118/119 From a 1950s milk bar: bar stools in Craig Port's kitchen. *Provenant d'un milk-bar des années 50 : des tabourets de bar dans la cuisine de Craig Port.* Aus einer Milchbar der 50er-Jahre: Barhocker in der Küche von Craig Port.

120/121 Neat and tidy: Craig Port's simple bedroom. *Bien rangée : la sobre chambre à coucher de Craig Port.* Aufgeräumt: Das schlichte Schlafzimmer von Craig Port.

122/123 Mirror, mirror on the wall: Craig Port's office. *Miroir, mon beau miroir : le bureau de Craig Port.* Spieglein, Spieglein an der Wand: Im Büro von Craig Port.

124/125   Centre of the house: the kitchen in Gapad Cottage, Greyton. *Le cœur de la maison : la cuisine de Gapad Cottage, Greyton.* Der Mittelpunkt des Hauses: Die Küche des Gapad Cottages, Greyton.

126/127   Good living: Jonathan Green and Marina Pretorius' salon, Greyton. *Vivre dans le beau : le salon de Jonathan Green et Marina Pretorius, Greyton.* Schöner wohnen: Der Salon von Jonathan Green und Marina Pretorius, Greyton.

128/129   Plain black: a varnished iron bed in the home of Jonathan Green and Marina Pretorius. *Sobre et noir : un lit en fer laqué chez Jonathan Green et Marina Pretorius.* Schlicht schwarz: Ein lackiertes Eisenbett bei Jonathan Green und Marina Pretorius.

130/131   Under flags: a club-like salon in "Meerlust" house, Stellenbosch. *Sous les drapeaux : salon de type club, dans la maison « Meerlust », à Stellenbosch.* Unter den Flaggen: Der clubähnliche Salon des Hauses »Meerlust«, Stellenbosch.

132/133   Fully equipped: the inviting kitchen at "Meerlust". *Parfaitement équipée : la cuisine conviviale de « Meerlust ».* Für alle Fälle gerüstet: Die einladende Küche von »Meerlust«.

"…A bag of lavender trimmed with velvet forget-me-nots hung from the upright hinge of the adjustable mirror of the dressing-table…"

Nadine Gordimer, in *July's People*

«…Un sac de lavande, orné de myosotis veloutés, était suspendu à la charnière verticale du miroir réglable de la coiffeuse…»

Nadine Gordimer, dans *Ceux de July*

»…Ein Lavendelbeutel, verziert mit Vergissmeinnicht aus Samt, hing an dem senkrechten Scharnier des verstellbaren Spiegels der Frisierkommode…«

Nadine Gordimer, in *July's Leute*

DETAILS
Détails Details

ESTHER Mahlangu

1993

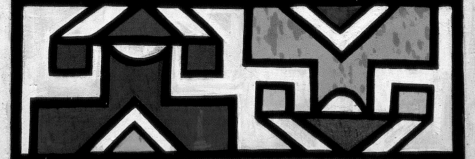

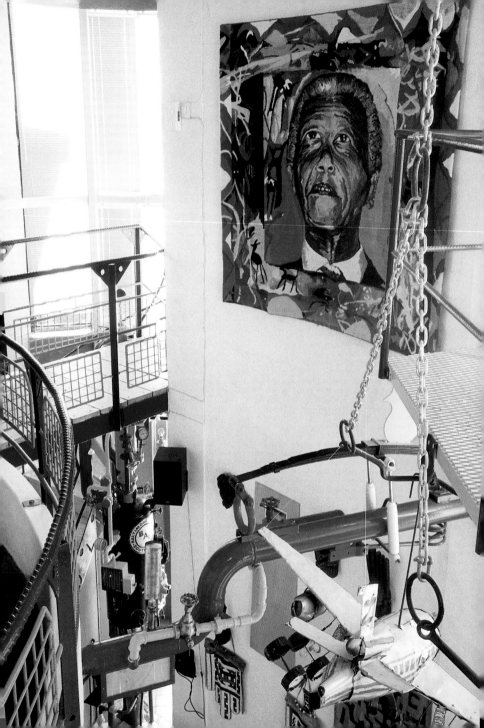

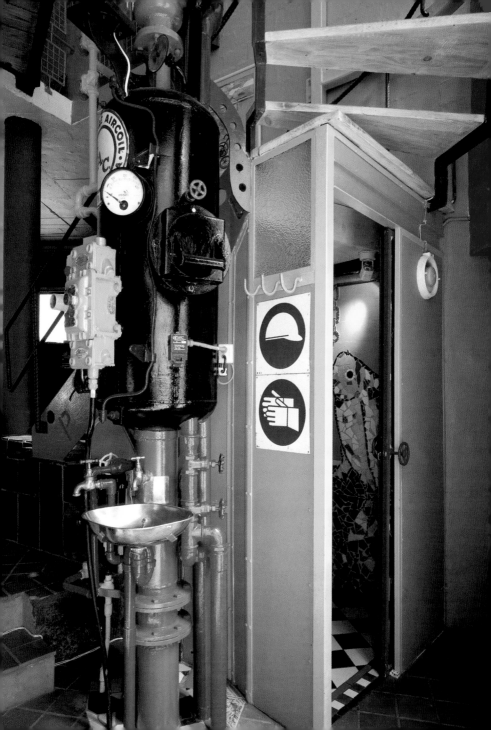

140 Mask-like: accessories at Camp 5, Makalali. *Comme des masques : accessoires au Camp 5, Makalali.* Maskenhaft: Accessoires im Camp 5, Makalali.

142 Showering al fresco: open-air bathroom at the private Lutopi lodge. *Douche en plein air : la salle de bains découverte du lodge privé Lutopi.* Freiluftdusche: Das Open-air-Bad der Privatlodge Lutopi.

143 Radiant white: the bath tub at the private Lutopi lodge. *Blanc rayonnant : la baignoire du lodge privé Lutopi.* Strahlend weiß: Die Badewanne der Privatlodge Lutopi.

144 Load-bearing role: a tree integrated into Casa Rech. *Rôle porteur : arbre intégré à la construction de la Casa Rech.* Tragende Rolle: Ein in den Bau der Casa Rech intergrierter Baum.

146 Ethno-design and modern lamps: in Casa Rech, Johannesburg. *Ethno design et lampes modernes : la Casa Rech, Johannesburg.* Ethnodesign und moderne Lampen: In der Casa Rech, Johannesburg.

147 Giver of warmth: the fireplace at Casa Rech. *Source de chaleur : la cheminée de la Casa Rech.* Wärme spendend: Der Kamin in der Casa Rech.

148 Family portraits: in the house of artist Louise Hennigs, Cape Town. *Galerie des aïeux : dans la maison de l'artiste Louise Hennigs, Le Cap.* Ahnengalerie: Im Haus der Künstlerin Louise Hennigs, Kapstadt.

150 Formal beauty: sofa under a Trevor Dykman lamp. *Formes parfaites : un canapé sous un luminaire de Trevor Dykman.* Formvollendet: Ein Kanapee unter einer Leuchte von Trevor Dykman.

151 Trophies: antelope antlers on the wall of Louise Hennigs' house. *Trophées : bois d'antilope en décoration murale, chez Louise Hennigs.* Trophäen: Antilopengeweihe als Wandschmuck, bei Louise Hennigs.

152 Towering: tree sculpture at Jean-Marc Lederman's pool, Llandudno. *Vers le ciel : sculpture arborée près de la piscine de Jean-Marc Lederman, Llandudno.* In den Himmel ragend: Baumskulptur am Pool von Jean-Marc Lederman, Llandudno.

154 Towards the sun: the house of Shahn and Alice Rowe, Johannesburg. *Rayon de soleil : dans la maison de Shahn et Alice Rowe, Johannesburg.* Der Sonne entgegen: Im Haus von Shahn und Alice Rowe, Johannesburg.

155 A hint of wild life: porcupine quills at Louise Hennigs' house. *La faune sauvage est toute proche : les piquants d'un porc-épic, chez Louise Hennigs.* Hinweise aufs nahe Wildlife: Stacheln von Stachelschweinen, bei Louise Hennigs.

156 A small paradise: open-air shower surrounded by roses at Louise Hennigs' house. *Petit paradis : la douche en plein air entourée de roses, chez Louise Hennigs.* Ein kleines Paradies: Die Open-air-Dusche im Rosenspalier, bei Louise Hennigs.

158 Heavenly colours: ceiling lighting in Shahn and Alice Rowe's bathroom. *Les couleurs du ciel : lumière de plafond dans la salle de bains de Shahn et Alice Rowe.* Die Farben des Himmels: Deckenlicht im Bad von Shahn und Alice Rowe.

159 Maritime inspiration: Shahn and Alice Rowe's bathtub. *Se laisser couler, tout simplement : la baignoire d'inspiration maritime de Shahn et Alice Rowe.* Einfach abtauchen: Die maritim inspirierte Wanne von Shahn und Alice Rowe.

160 Sparkling shades of blue: even in the Rowe's toilet. *Petit coin tranquille : même les toilettes des Rowe brillent dans des tons bleus.* Stilles Örtchen: Auch die Toilette der Rowes leuchtet in Blautönen.

162 Still-life in bamboo: at Malcolm Kluk's house, Cape Town. *Nature morte aux bambous : dans la maison de Malcolm Kluk, Le Cap.* Stillleben mit Bambus: Im Haus von Malcolm Kluk, Kapstadt.

163 Hope: an appeal on a wall in Malcolm Kluk's house. *Principe espérance: appel sur un mur dans la maison de Malcolm Kluk.* Das Prinzip Hoffnung: Appell an einer Wand im Haus von Malcolm Kluk.

164 Stacked: Malcolm Kluk's constantly growing library. *Empilement : la bibliothèque toujours plus riche de Malcolm Kluk.* Gestapelt: Die ständig wachsende Bibliothek von Malcolm Kluk.

166 Song of the sirens: Beezy Bailey's pool, Cape Town. *Le chant des sirènes : la piscine de Beezy Bailey, Le Cap.* Sirenengesänge unter Wasser: Der Pool von Beezy Bailey, Kapstadt.

167 Sweet dreams: light switch in Malcolm Kluk's bedroom. *Doux rêves : interrupteur dans la chambre à coucher de Malcolm Kluk.* Süße Träume: Lichtschalter im Schlafzimmer von Malcolm Kluk.

168 Fleamarket treasures: an abundantly decorated dining table. *Trésors de la brocante : décoration exubérante de la table.* Schätze vom Flohmarkt: Am üppig dekorierten Esstisch.

170 Manor house kitsch: the loving decor at Gapad Cottage. *Kitsch de maison de campagne : Coin décoré avec amour Gapad Cottage.* Landhauskitsch: Liebevolle Dekoration im Gapad Cottage.

171 Art in wood: details in Gapad Cottage. *Bois sculpté : détails de Gapad Cottage.* Kunst aus Holz: Details im Gapad Cottage.

173 Dropping anchor: a model ship in Jonathan Green and Marina Pretorius' house. *A bon port : maquette de bateau chez Jonathan Green et Marina Pretorius, Greyton.* Vor Anker gegangen: Ein Schiffsmodell bei Jonathan Green und Marina Pretorius, Greyton.

174/175 Nicely curved: stucco at the time-honoured "Meerlust" estate, Stellenbosch. *Belles volutes : stuc dans la propriété ancestrale de « Meerlust », à Stellenbosch.* Schön geschwungen: Stuck am altehrwürdigen Anwesen »Meerlust«, Stellenbosch.

176 Reflections: at the idyllic pond of Gapad Cottage, Greyton. *Reflets dans l'eau : l'étang idyllique du Gapad Cottage, Greyton.* Im Wasser gespiegelt: Am idyllischen Teich des Gapad Cottage, Greyton.

178/179 Ndebele colours: works by the famous artist Esther Mahlangu. *Les couleurs des Ndebele : œuvres de la célèbre artiste Esther Mahlangu.* Die Farben der Ndebele: Werke der berühmten Künstlerin Esther Mahlangu.

180 Safe? An electric socket in a Cape Town township. *Sécurité assurée ? Une prise électrique dans les bidonvilles du Cap.* Gut gesichert? Steckdose in den Townships von Kapstadt.

182 Place of honour: a portrait of Nelson Mandela. *À la place d'honneur : un portrait de Nelson Mandela.* Ehrenplatz: Ein Portrait von Nelson Mandela.

183 Colourful chaos: in Willie Bester's cellar. *Un chantier haut en couleurs : la cave de Willie Bester.* Buntes Baustellenflair: Im Keller von Willie Bester.

184 A cordial welcome: in front of a small shop in a Cape Town township. *Bienvenue : devant une petite boutique des bidonvilles du Cap.* Herzlich willkommen: Vor einem kleinen Laden in den Townships von Kapstadt.

186 Upside down: sculptures in Beezy Bailey's house, Cape Town. *Tête-bêche : sculptures dans la maison de Beezy Bailey, Le Cap.* Auf den Kopf gestellt: Skulpturen im Haus von Beezy Bailey, Kapstadt.

187 Bathroom knicksknacks: at the home of Tracy Rushmere and Peter Maltbie. *Bric-à-brac autour de la baignoire : affiche et personnages de Tracy Rushmere et Peter Maltbie.* Nippes an der Badewanne: Poster und Plastik bei Tracy Rushmere und Peter Maltbie.

The Hotelbook. Great Escapes Africa Shelley-Maree Cassidy / Ed. Angelika Taschen / Hardcover, 400 pp. / € 29.99 / $ 39.99 / £ 19.99 / ¥ 5.900

Inside Africa Ed. Angelika Taschen / Deidi von Schaewen / Hardcover, 2 volumes, 912 pp. / € 99.99 / $ 125 / £ 69.99 / ¥ 15.000

"In two volumes, this is a remarkable, colossal undertaking – more than simply a visual source book." —House & Garden, London, on Inside Africa

"Buy them all and add some pleasure to your life."

African Style
Ed. Angelika Taschen

Alchemy & Mysticism
Alexander Roob

All-American Ads 40s
Ed. Jim Heimann

All-American Ads 50s
Ed. Jim Heimann

All-American Ads 60s
Ed. Jim Heimann

American Indian
Dr. Sonja Schierle

Angels
Gilles Néret

Architecture Now!
Ed. Philip Jodidio

Art Now
Eds. Burkhard Riemschneider, Uta Grosenick

Atget's Paris
Ed. Hans Christian Adam

Berlin Style
Ed. Angelika Taschen

Cars of the 50s
Ed. Jim Heimann, Tony Thacker

Cars of the 60s
Ed. Jim Heimann, Tony Thacker

Cars of the 70s
Ed. Jim Heimann, Tony Thacker

Chairs
Charlotte & Peter Fiell

Christmas
Ed. Jim Heimann, Steven Heller

Classic Rock Covers
Ed. Michael Ochs

Design Handbook
Charlotte & Peter Fiell

Design of the 20th Century
Charlotte & Peter Fiell

Design for the 21st Century
Charlotte & Peter Fiell

Devils
Gilles Néret

Digital Beauties
Ed. Julius Wiedemann

Robert Doisneau
Ed. Jean-Claude Gautrand

East German Design
Ralf Ulrich / Photos: Ernst Hedler

Egypt Style
Ed. Angelika Taschen

Encyclopaedia Anatomica
Ed. Museo La Specola Florence

M.C. Escher

Fashion
Ed. The Kyoto Costume Institute

Fashion Now!
Ed. Terry Jones, Susie Rushton

Fruit
Ed. George Brookshaw, Uta Pellgrü-Gagel

HR Giger
HR Giger

Grand Tour
Harry Seidler

Graphic Design
Eds. Charlotte & Peter Fiell

Greece Style
Ed. Angelika Taschen

Halloween
Ed. Jim Heimann, Steven Heller

Havana Style
Ed. Angelika Taschen

Homo Art
Gilles Néret

Hot Rods
Ed. Coco Shinomiya, Tony Thacker

Hula
Ed. Jim Heimann

Indian Style
Ed. Angelika Taschen

India Bazaar
Samantha Harrison, Bari Kumar

Industrial Design
Charlotte & Peter Fiell

Japanese Beauties
Ed. Alex Gross

Krazy Kids' Food
Eds. Steve Roden, Dan Goodsell

Las Vegas
Ed. Jim Heimann, W. R. Wilkerson III

London Style
Ed. Angelika Taschen

Mexicana
Ed. Jim Heimann

Mexico Style
Ed. Angelika Taschen

Morocco Style
Ed. Angelika Taschen

Starck
Philippe Starck

New York Style
Ed. Angelika Taschen

Paris Style
Ed. Angelika Taschen

Penguin
Frans Lanting

20th Century Photography
Museum Ludwig Cologne

Photo Icons I
Hans-Michael Koetzle

Photo Icons II
Hans-Michael Koetzle

Pierre et Gilles
Eric Troncy

Provence Style
Ed. Angelika Taschen

Robots & Spaceships
Ed. Teruhisa Kitahara

Safari Style
Ed. Angelika Taschen

Seaside Style
Ed. Angelika Taschen

Albertus Seba. Butterflies
Irmgard Müsch

Albertus Seba. Shells & Corals
Irmgard Müsch

Signs
Ed. Julius Wiedeman

South African Style
Ed. Angelika Taschen

Starck
Philippe Starck

Surfing
Ed. Jim Heimann

Sweden Style
Ed. Angelika Taschen

Sydney Style
Ed. Angelika Taschen

Tattoos
Ed. Henk Schiffmacher

Tiffany
Jacob Baal-Teshuva

Tiki Style
Sven Kirsten

Tuscany Style
Ed. Angelika Taschen

Valentines
Ed. Jim Heimann, Steven Heller

Web Design: Best Studios
Ed. Julius Wiedemann

Web Design: Flash Sites
Ed. Julius Wiedemann

Web Design: Portfolios
Ed. Julius Wiedemann

Women Artists in the 20th and 21st Century
Ed. Uta Grosenick

ICONS